TIME FLIES
Written by PJ Harris & Illustrated by Dylan Fant

Published through Opus Self-Publishing Services
Located at:
Politics and Prose Bookstore
5015 Connecticut Ave. NW
Washington, D.C. 20008
www.politics-prose.com // (202) 364-1919

This book was created for kids of all ages,
with a gentle reminder tucked into its pages,
that no matter the stage of your life you now live in,
remember to cherish the time you are given.

A very young child,
precocious and wild,
wished to live happy and free.

So he climbed up the mount,
determined to seek out
the person he wanted to see.

The eager young boy
set out to employ
the help of the kind Wise One.

WISE ONE
YONDER

He knocked on the door
and sat on the floor,
waiting for the Wise One to come.

After a long time,
the Wise One arrived,
and let the young child inside.

She said, "Go on, speak!
Tell me what you seek?"
And quite eager to oblige,
He said...

"Please, could you tell me just who I should be,
to live life happy and well?"

The Wise One replied, with a look in her eyes,
"That answer only Time can tell."

The child did not like
that answer one mite,
for he knew not where to find...

...that elusive old puck,
who'd forever been stuck
with the nickname of 'Old Father Time.'

So the child then said to the Wise One instead,
"Can you tell me where Time dwells?"

The Wise One replied, the same look in her eyes,
"I don't know, you should go ask the Well."

The boy left the house and then ventured out
to find the Wishing Well.

If anyone knew the next thing to do,
it was the Well who could tell.

Before he got there, something in the air
kept him away from his search.

High up in the sky, dark battled with light,
both fighting to keep their perch.

"Help!" cried out the Sun, who was the sole one
fighting the Dark for the sky's fate.

And then, even though he wished he could go,
he figured the Well could wait.

He picked up a stone, threw it where the Sun shone,
and the Sun filled it up with light.

The Sun said, "Brilliant, you are! We'll call this a star!"
and hurled the bright stone at the night.

It shattered the night, filling it with light,
and the Sun was very much pleased.

As he sunk away,
the Sun said, clear as day,
"Look to the stars in your need!"

And at the Sun's last word, the youth remembered
that he wished to see the Well.

But now in the night he feared that he might
not see in the dark very well.

But the stars said, "Don't fear! For we are right here
to lead you down to the Well."

They led him past a mill, and over a hill,
and finally down through a dell.

"Thanks!" said the young man, as he quickly ran
to the place where the stars led.

The Well was right there, under the night air,
so he approached it and said...

"I wish you'd tell me just who I should be
to live life happy and free?"

But when it said nothing,
the young man got testy,
and yelled at at the Well, "Answer Me!"

And it said...
"Your answer can't come from a Well.
That answer only Time can tell."

"I knew that!" he said, and then asked instead,
"Where is it that Time resides?"

"The forest tonight, but leaves at daylight.
I must warn you that TIME FLIES!"

The man understood.
He ran to the woods,
in search of Old Father Time.

But before he knew it,
he slipped in a pit
filled up with water and slime.

"Sorry about that,"
 said the sopping vat,
"but I've been crying, you see?"

"I'm filled up with tears because my love, I fear,
won't so much as look at me."

"I love that dear Tree. She won't notice me.
Help me before it's too late!"

And then, even though he wished he could go,
he figured even Time could wait."

So he found a seed
that he then buried,
and watered it with the Lake's tears.

Almost instantly,
right under the Tree,
a bright red flower appeared.

"That's precious, you know! We'll call this a rose!"
The Lake said as the Tree took notice.

Tree looked at the rose, saw the love that it showed,
and bent to give the Lake a kiss.

The grown man was pleased to see his good deed,
but then he set off again.

And then, finally, he saw, happily,
Time right around the riverbend.

And Time said...

"Hello there, my friend, and what can I do
to help a man as great as you?"

"A man?" he then mused, a little confused
by the words of Father Time.

But he saw his hands,
worn by dirt and sand,
were now looking past their prime.

He felt very strange,
as if something changed,
when he asked, "Who should I be?"

Time gave him a look
he must have mistook
for something like sympathy.

You put light in the dark,

you put love in a heart.
You're a wonder, and you
should be pleased."

"I wish you'd have known,
the whole while you've grown,
to stop and smell the roses.

Stop and look at the stars,
and how precious you are.
I'd have suggested a few doses...

... of peace and perspective,
a whole new directive,
to treat every day as sublime.

To be grateful for you, and for all you can do,

and to never,

not ever,

chase Time."

And then Time was gone... The old man looked on,
wondering if he'd missed out
on adventure, or love, or all the above.
And he realized what life was about...

He never chased after Time again.

And that, my young friend, is the end.